ESSENTIAL LIBRARY OF THE
INFORMATION AGE

NET NEUTRALITY

by Melissa Higgins and Michael Regan

CONTENT CONSULTANT

Dr. Daniel A. Lyons

Associate Professor of Law

Boston College Law School

Essential Library

An Imprint of Abdo Publishing | abdopublishing.com

abdopublishing.com

Published by Abdo Publishing, a division of ABDO, PO Box 398166, Minneapolis, Minnesota 55439. Copyright © 2017 by Abdo Consulting Group, Inc. International copyrights reserved in all countries. No part of this book may be reproduced in any form without written permission from the publisher. Essential Library™ is a trademark and logo of Abdo Publishing.

Printed in the United States of America, North Mankato, Minnesota
052016
092016

THIS BOOK CONTAINS
RECYCLED MATERIALS

Cover Photo: Red Line Editorial
Interior Photos: Frederick M. Brown/Getty Images, 5; Mark Van Scyoc/Shutterstock Images, 7; Alexey Boldin/Shutterstock Images, 11; iStockphoto, 15, 27; Lennart Preiss/Photothek/Getty Images, 17; Toby Jorrin/AP Images, 20; Michael Smith/Getty Images, 23; Ron Edmonds/AP Images, 28; Mark Lennihan/AP Images, 31; Kevin P. Casey/AP Images, 35; Richard B. Levine/Newscom, 39; Karen Bleier/AFP/Getty Images, 41; Shutterstock Images, 44; Kimberly White/Getty Images, 47; Scott J. Ferrell/Congressional Quarterly/Newscom, 50; Steve Rhodes/Demotix/Corbis, 53; George Frey/Reuters/Corbis, 57; Scott J. Ferrell/Congressional Quarterly/Getty Images, 59, 88; Steven Senne/AP Images, 62; Bob Daemmrich/Corbis, 65; Matt Rourke/AP Images, 69; Christopher Lane/ AP Images for The New Yorker/AP Images, 71; Aijaz Rahi/AP Images, 74, 80; Sean Pavone/ Shutterstock Images, 77; Craig Mitchelldyer/Getty Images, 83; Daniel Acker/Bloomberg/Getty Images, 87; Mark Wilson/Getty Images, 92; Press Trust of India/AP Images, 99

Editor: Arnold Ringstad
Series Designer: Craig Hinton

Publisher's Cataloging in Publication Data

Names: Higgins, Melissa, author. | Regan, Michael, author.
Title: Net neutrality / by Melissa Higgins and Michael Regan.
Description: Minneapolis, MN : Abdo Publishing, [2017] | Series: Essential library
    of the information age | Includes bibliographical references and index.
Identifiers: LCCN 2015960312 | ISBN 9781680782868 (lib. bdg.) |
    ISBN 9781680774757 (ebook)
Subjects: LCSH: Telecommunication policy--Juvenile literature. | Network
    neutrality--Juvenile literature. | Internet--Juvenile literature.
Classification: DDC 384.3--dc23
LC record available at http://lccn.loc.gov/2015960312

CONTENTS

CHAPTER 1

ANYTHING BUT NEUTRAL

On June 1, 2014, television host John Oliver spoke about net neutrality for 13 minutes on his comedy and news show, *Last Week Tonight*. Net neutrality is the idea that Internet service providers (ISPs) should give customers equal access to all legal websites and content. In addition, ISPs should not be able to charge certain content providers more money for faster speeds. The subject of net neutrality may sound technical and abstract, but it is incredibly important in our modern connected world.

During the *Last Week Tonight* segment, Oliver noted that the Federal Communications Commission (FCC) was proposing new rules for the Internet. The FCC was debating whether to adopt a two-tiered Internet streaming system in which ISPs—such as Comcast and Verizon—would be permitted to charge content providers—such as Netflix and Google—an extra fee for faster and more reliable service. Oliver argued that although Netflix and Google could afford these higher fees, the new rules would

Since launching the show in April 2014, John Oliver has used *Last Week Tonight* to draw attention to important issues in the news.

put small content providers and start-up web companies at an unfair disadvantage.

Oliver said, "Ending net neutrality would allow big companies to buy their way into the fast lane, leaving everyone else in the slow lane."[1] He then pointed to studies showing the major ISPs were some of the most disliked companies in the United States and had a virtual monopoly on providing Internet service. He alleged the ISPs do not have consumers' best interests in mind. At the end of the segment, Oliver mentioned that the FCC was currently inviting public comments about net neutrality. He rallied Internet users to send their opinions to the FCC website, telling them to "focus your indiscriminate rage in a useful direction."[2]

One million viewers saw the *Last Week Tonight* segment on net neutrality during its first airing. It was then shared widely on social

The FCC, headquartered in Washington, DC, is an agency responsible for regulating communications of many different kinds.

media networks such as Twitter and Facebook. On June 2, 2014, the day after Oliver's segment, the FCC's online public comment system crashed under heavy traffic. More than 4 million people filed public comments.[3] Only 1 percent of them were opposed to net neutrality enforcement.[4]

Many credited this outpouring of public opinion with helping to influence the FCC's February 26, 2015, decision to drop its two-tier plan. Aram Sinnreich, professor of journalism at Rutgers University, said in an interview, "The democratic support for this decision relied heavily on citing the millions of citizen comments submitted via the FCC's website, and those comments were overwhelmingly inspired, directly and indirectly, by Oliver's advocacy."[5]

PASSIONATE OPINIONS

At the opening of his segment on net neutrality, Oliver admitted that the topic was so dull he would rather "listen to a pair of [pants] tell me about the weird dream it had."[6] So how does the topic inspire such passions?

For supporters of net neutrality, the debate centers on equal Internet access for businesses and for the public. Supporters include consumer advocates, small web companies, and larger web companies that deliver content over the Internet. They argue that even the smallest business using the Internet, regardless of how much money it has, should have the same opportunity for success as a larger company has. That opportunity is reduced if the small company cannot afford to pay for fast speeds. Net neutrality supporters say the public should have access without being blocked from certain websites or having speeds purposely manipulated.

On the other side of the net neutrality argument are individuals who oppose government regulations, as well as a group of cable and telecom companies. These companies have spent years and billions of dollars building high-speed Internet networks and contend there is nothing wrong with creating Internet fast lanes. They say the Internet will remain open under such a structure, and consumers will not be blocked from accessing any content. Further, these opponents contend

> ❝ When you say fast lane and slow lane, it's a good illustration. But what you should really be talking about is a fast lane for everybody and a hyper-speed lane for others. ❞ [7]
>
> —George Foote, telecommunications lawyer

that government regulations deter investment in improving the Internet. They say that regulations could also harm innovation by preventing the development of services that take advantage of Internet fast lanes. Some companies argue the FCC should have no legal right to regulate them at all.

CONFUSING POLICIES AND QUESTIONS

Since the World Wide Web began growing in popularity and importance in the early 1990s, US policymakers have struggled with regulating the Internet. Members of Congress and the FCC have tried to strike a balance between protecting consumer and business access while being fair to ISPs. From the FCC's earliest ruling on Internet regulation in 2002, the issue has been rocked on a seesaw of government rulings and court decisions. These developments are complicated by the technical nature of the Internet.

For some, the question of net neutrality boils down to ownership. Is the Internet

NOT A NEW CONCEPT

The concept of net neutrality goes back as far as 1888. Almon Brown Strowger, an undertaker, became fed up with a phone operator, the wife of a rival mortician. She kept redirecting calls meant for him to other people named Strowger so he would lose business. As a solution, Strowger invented the first automatic telephone exchange that routed calls without needing a human operator. All calls were treated equally and could be made without interference.

The Internet has become an indispensable tool for education, work, and leisure, making its regulation an issue that affects billions of people around the world.

owned by the government, which regulates it? Is it owned by the people who use it? Or is it owned by the companies that provide access to it? Proponents of net neutrality say there are too few

Proponents of net neutrality include both Internet startup companies and large Internet content providers. These major providers include Netflix, Apple, eBay, Twitter, Facebook, Vimeo, Google, and Amazon.com. Other groups in favor include consumer advocacy and human rights organizations, such as Free Press, Common Cause, Public Knowledge, and Fight for the Future. President Barack Obama and many Democratic members of Congress are also in favor of net neutrality.

Those against net neutrality regulation include large ISPs, such as Comcast, Time Warner Cable, Cox, AT&T, and Verizon. Also opposed to net neutrality are industry advocacy groups, such as the US Telecom Association and the National Cable & Telecommunications Association, and think tanks, such as the Free State Foundation and the Information Technology and Innovation Foundation. Many Republicans are also against the idea of adding extra rules and regulations for businesses, as are some large tech companies, including Intel, IBM, Qualcomm, and Cisco.

companies providing access to the Internet. They argue this problem is made worse when large companies purchase or merge with competitors. They believe that without competition, these companies wield too much power and control, and the results are high costs, poor service, and a lack of choice. They contend that because of these factors, the FCC must regulate ISPs to maintain an open Internet.

Under increasing pressure from net neutrality proponents, including President Barack Obama, the FCC ruled in 2015 that the Internet was a public utility subject to strong regulations. The ruling raised alarms for critics who fear government bureaucracy and oversight will have a negative effect on technology

> **'Net neutrality'** has been built into the fabric of the Internet since its creation—but it is also a principle that we cannot take for granted. We cannot allow Internet Service Providers (ISPs) to restrict the best access or to pick winners and losers in the online marketplace for service and ideas. [8]
>
> —President Barack Obama, in a November 10, 2014, statement

business investment. The FCC's 2015 decision was quickly challenged with lawsuits and proposed legislation.

The issue of net neutrality is not limited to the United States. Governments around the globe are struggling with similar questions and finding different types of solutions. The story of net neutrality is far from over.

CHAPTER 2

FROM THE EARLY INTERNET TO BROADBAND

A free and open Internet, where a user can do, see, and create online without restriction, was the ideal goal when the Internet was under development from the 1960s through the mid-1990s. At first, the US government took a hands-off approach to regulating the fledgling Internet. It believed that was the best way for users to develop innovative technologies, applications, and products. And unlike the telephone business, in which the company AT&T had a monopoly through most of the 1900s, the early Internet and Web were full of healthy competition.

INTERNET STRUCTURE

The Internet—a global network of connected computer networks—was originally funded by the US government in the 1960s and was limited to university research, education, and government services. When easy access to the Internet became available in 1990 through the World Wide Web, Internet usage

The Internet has opened up new lines of communication that crisscross the globe. Regulating these connections is a controversial issue.

exploded and attracted high interest from both individuals and businesses. In 1995, the government discontinued its funding of Internet infrastructure. All Internet traffic now had to go through commercial networks.

The structure of the Internet consists of three parts. One is the Internet backbone. These are large-capacity, high-speed data networks, usually made up of fiber optic lines, that interconnect with each other. Often called the Internet highway or "pipes," they are owned and operated by universities, private companies (including some ISPs), the military, and governments. A second part of the Internet is ISPs. ISPs use the backbone to access the Internet, and they provide the "little pipes" or "last mile" of cables and wires that enter homes and businesses and connect individual users to the Internet. A third part of the Internet is content providers, which make applications and products for Internet users. To reach users, content providers connect to ISPs so they can access the ISP's "last mile" lines.

Fiber optic backbone lines typically run underground.

The control of the connection points between these parts is where the net neutrality battle lies. How they are regulated has become a point of contention between government agencies, politicians, large and small corporations, and individual users of the Internet. The battle can trace its history to one very old English law and one very large American company.

COMMON CARRIER AND TELECOMMUNICATIONS

A key element of net neutrality is a legal concept called "common carrier." In 1701, an English court ruled certain public businesses that work in the public interest could not discriminate against any member of the public who wanted to use that service. For example, a stagecoach company serving the public could not refuse to transport goods for a person if that person had the money to pay and the company had room on its wagon. This common-carriage principle became part of the American legal system and was applied to railroads, other types of transportation, and communications media.

The telecommunications industry presents a unique challenge. Installing phone lines requires the approval of federal, state, and local governments, because poles and wires cross through, under, and over land and roads that are publicly owned. Plus, installing all of those poles, wires, and cables requires a huge investment. Very few companies are willing to invest in that kind of infrastructure unless they can be assured of a profit. For these reasons, in 1913 the US government allowed a single company, American Telephone and Telegraph (AT&T), to provide telephone service for the entire country. This was a legal monopoly. The government tasked the FCC and state public utility commissions with regulating AT&T to keep the company from using unfair business practices.

AT&T was not prevented from selling products related to the telephone system, including the telephones themselves. It used its monopoly power to dominate these markets. In 1984, after a decade of antitrust litigation, the US government forced AT&T to

AT&T had a monopoly in many areas associated with telecommunications, including telephone handsets. In the 1960s, an entrepreneur named Thomas Carter brought a successful lawsuit against the company. He wanted to sell his own model of cordless phone. Bowing to that lawsuit, the FCC began allowing other companies to offer phones, beginning in 1968. That ruling then led to the sale of other phone-related devices, including answering machines, fax machines, and eventually computer modems. The FCC hoped the increased competition might change AT&T's monopolistic behavior, but that did not happen. In 1974, President Gerald Ford's administration filed an antitrust lawsuit against the company. AT&T was forced to split into its parent company of AT&T and seven new regional telephone companies: Ameritech, Bell Atlantic, BellSouth, NYNEX, Pacific Telesis, Southwestern Bell, and US West.

split up its company to increase market competition. The story of AT&T would have an eventual effect on net neutrality.

THE EARLY INTERNET

The first ISP provided service for customers in 1989, the same year the World Wide Web was created. Customers accessed the Internet through dial-up connections, which operated over existing phone lines. If AT&T had still been a monopoly during the rise of the Internet, some experts believe it would have seen the Internet as a threat and hampered its growth by not letting ISPs use its lines. Net neutrality was not an issue at the time, because phone companies had to comply with common carrier rules allowing all ISPs—even competing ones—access to their phone lines. Open access to the Internet during its early years allowed for the rapid expansion of content and applications. Engineer Vint Cerf, sometimes called

AT&T's split led the government to reconsider allowing legal communications monopolies.

the "father of the Internet," said these early years of common carrier regulations allowed Internet users to "unleash their creative, innovative, and inspired . . . ideas . . . without artificial barriers erected by the telephone companies."[1]

The first connections over telephone dial-up systems were extremely slow compared to today's cable, fiber-optic, satellite, and digital subscriber line (DSL) broadband connections. Broadband connections are defined as operating at speeds greater than 25 megabits per second (Mbps). From 1984 through 1992, cable companies invested $15 billion in wiring American homes for cable TV. Between 1996 and 2002, they invested $65 billion more to build higher-capacity fiber optic and coaxial cable broadband networks—the cables that carried the Internet.[2] Broadband Internet first came to North American homes in 1996 when Rogers Communications began cable modem service in Canada. Internet users began moving from dial-up services to broadband and enjoying speeds 50 to 100 times faster. Between 2000 and 2001, broadband subscriptions rose more than 50 percent in US households.[3] With the exception of DSL, none of the emerging broadband services used telephone lines.

Because phone-line–based ISPs and DSL connections were subject to common carrier rules relating to the telephone, a question arose: Should non–phone-line broadband services, such as cable and fiber optics, be subject to the same common carrier rules because they provided essentially the same service? Large ISPs emphatically said no. They had invested billions of dollars in developing broadband infrastructure— much like AT&T had done with phone lines in the 1900s—and

VINT CERF, FATHER OF THE INTERNET

Vint Cerf, along with Robert Kahn, is known as one of the "fathers of the Internet" for developing the protocols, or procedures, that define how information moves on the Internet. In 1997, Cerf was awarded the US National Medal of Technology by President Bill Clinton. In 2004, he was awarded the ACM Alan M. Turing award, known as the "Nobel Prize of Computer Science." In 2005, he was awarded the Presidential Medal of Freedom by President George W. Bush.

Cable television and Internet data are transmitted through copper wires surrounded by material that insulates and protects them. Fiber optic cables are made of very thin strands of glass or plastic that carry digital information on a beam of light. Dial-up and DSL Internet connections use copper wire telephone lines. Phone lines traditionally transmit sound, which is an analog signal. Because computers only understand digital signals, dial-up connections use devices called modems to translate from analog to digital. In contrast, DSL signals are delivered across phone lines digitally. Digital signals can be sent more quickly than analog ones. This is why DSL speeds are much faster than dial-up.

they did not think it was fair that other companies should be allowed free access to their networks. But smaller ISPs, many content providers, and users disagreed. They argued that large ISPs were quickly developing monopolies on the networks that provided access to users. The US Congress and the FCC, both under heavy lobbying from service and content providers, stepped in to resolve the disagreement.

THE TELECOMMUNICATIONS ACT OF 1996 AND THE 2002 FCC RULING

The US Congress made a distinction between a "telecommunications service" and an "information service" in the Telecommunications Act of 1996. The act defined a *telecommunications service* as a service that transmits a user's information from one place to another without changing the content or form of the information. An example of this would be a person's voice in a phone call. On the other hand, the act defined

Enormous investments in materials and labor are needed to set up broadband infrastructure.

an *information service* as a service that offers a user the capability to generate, store, or process, or make available information via telecommunications. Google's search engine is an example of an information service. The act, passed by a majority-Republican Congress and signed into law by Democratic president Bill Clinton, stated it would "preserve the vibrant and competitive free market that presently exists for the Internet and other interactive computer services, unfettered by Federal or State regulation."[4]

In late 1996, the cable company Comcast launched its first ISP broadband product. The company believed this was an information service under the Telecommunications Act, meaning it would not be subject to common-carrier rules. But when the law took effect, it was not clear whether non–phone-line ISPs were a telecommunications service or an information service. In 2002, an FCC ruling clarified this issue. The commission stated that cable broadband was indeed an information service, not a telecommunications service, and any ISP not using phone lines was therefore not subject to FCC common-carrier regulations.

Broadband companies were now no longer restricted by common-carrier requirements, which meant they could exclude any customer they wanted or refuse to let a competing ISP company use their infrastructure. By eliminating competition and decreasing government oversight, the FCC hoped its ruling would encourage ISPs to expand the expensive wiring and cables necessary to spread broadband service across the country. Although infrastructure did expand, another consequence of the 1996 Telecommunications Act and

> **"**The 'Common Carrier' regime has always acknowledged that providers can create different classes of service as long as they charge everyone who wants that class of service the same amount. . . . It wouldn't prevent Internet service providers from creating a fast lane in the first place. **"** [5]
>
> —Christopher Yoo, professor, University of Pennsylvania

2002 FCC ruling harkened back the days of giant AT&T. Small ISPs were now unable to operate on the big players' wires and cables, which meant competition in the broadband market decreased. With less competition came a lack of choice for consumers. Mergers of broadband companies into larger corporations decreased consumer choice even more. To many observers, it seemed that a few large companies now owned the Internet.

CHAPTER 3

ISPs VERSUS THE FCC

For many years, ISPs stuck to a single pricing system for content providers. Then, in 2005, YouTube came online and quickly grew in popularity. On-demand video began using enormous amounts of data, and evidence grew to suggest that some ISPs were now slowing and blocking traffic without telling customers. This caught the attention of the FCC.

FOUR PRINCIPLES OF THE OPEN INTERNET

After the 2002 FCC ruling defined cable ISPs as information services, backers of net neutrality argued for stronger broadband regulations. Meanwhile, opponents of net neutrality tried to get the FCC to reinforce its hands-off approach to the Internet. The general public was largely unaware of these battles over net neutrality.

In 2004, FCC chairman Michael Powell introduced four principles for ensuring net neutrality. He believed that consumers

The introduction of YouTube and other video streaming services led to a dramatic increase in the amount of data traveling through the infrastructure of the Internet.

YouTube Home

This week

Top rated

All

Autos & Vehicles

> **To realize the innovation dream that IP communications promises . . . we must ensure that a willing provider can reach a willing consumer over the broadband connection. Ensuring that consumers can obtain and use the content, applications, and devices they choose is critical to unlocking the vast potential of the Internet.** [1]
>
> —Michael Powell, FCC chairman, in a 2004 speech announcing the four principles of the open Internet

should be able to access whatever legal content they wanted; be able to run any computer programs they wanted; be allowed to attach any Internet connection devices they wanted in their homes; and be given meaningful information about their Internet service plans. Cable broadband services were not under FCC control at this time, because they had been classified as information services—not telecommunication services—under the FCC's 2002 ruling. But Powell's principles encouraged champions of net neutrality, as it now appeared the commission might be in the early stages of changing the Internet's classification.

BRAND X AND LOCAL CONTROL VERSUS BIG ISPs

Initially the FCC refused to decide whether broadband ISPs should be considered common carriers or merely information service providers. In a 1999 speech, FCC chairman William Kennard

Following his time as FCC chairman, Powell became a lobbyist for a major cable television trade group.

explained the agency sought to take a hands-off approach. He was worried that placing common carriage obligations and other regulations on a fledgling broadband industry might harm the Internet's development. But several local governments stepped into the regulatory vacuum caused by the FCC's indecision. Specifically, local franchising authorities had the authority to regulate cable services. They attempted to impose open access requirements on cable-based broadband providers. AT&T challenged one such restriction placed on it by the city of Portland, Oregon. The US Ninth Circuit Court sided with AT&T, finding that broadband service was not a cable service and, therefore, Portland lacked authority to impose open access restrictions. But the decision was not a complete victory for AT&T. The court concluded that cable broadband was best classified as a telecommunications service, which opened the door for the FCC or others to impose the same common-carrier restrictions that were traditionally placed on phone companies.

Now that the Ninth Circuit had forced its hand, the FCC abandoned its earlier strategy of inaction and ruled that, contrary to the court's decision, broadband service provided by cable modem was an information service under the Telecommunications Act. The US Supreme Court upheld that decision in June 2005 in *National Cable & Telecommunications Association v. Brand X*

Disputes over the common-carrier status of telecommunications lines led to changes in the industry.

Internet Services. Shortly thereafter, the FCC reclassified DSL as an information service as well. With these rulings, AT&T was freed of the obligation of sharing its cable and phone lines with other ISPs who sought to compete against it.

Following the *Brand X* decision, Ben Scott, the policy director for the organization Free Press, said, "The response of the telephone giants that control the DSL market will no doubt be to rush to the FCC and the Congress to demand their own exemption from open-access regulations."[2] And that is exactly what happened.

THE FCC GIVES AND TAKES

But in the same August 5, 2005, meeting at which it reclassified DSL as an information service, the FCC adopted Powell's four principles. It said ISPs should follow the four principles and treat companies and consumers equally. But it soon became clear that some large ISPs did not intend to follow the FCC's recommendations. In November 2007, Vuze Inc., a provider of self-published video content, filed a petition with the FCC complaining Comcast was abusing the FCC's "reasonable network management" principle by slowing and blocking Vuze traffic on the Internet.

A month earlier, an Associated Press article published in the *Washington Post* reported Comcast was blocking or slowing some customers trying to share files online. Nationwide tests performed by the Associated Press showed Comcast's interference with file sharing was "the most drastic example yet of data discrimination by a US Internet service provider."[3] The blocking or slowing of data appeared to target peer-to-peer (P2P) file sharing applications, such as BitTorrent. These services made up the majority of all Internet traffic. Comcast said it was managing its network traffic only during times of heavy usage. The company added that this was within its rights as an information service.

In April 2008, FCC chairman Kevin Martin testified before the US Senate Commerce, Science, and Transportation Committee. He said it seemed Comcast was blocking P2P traffic even during times when net traffic was not heavy, which was the opposite of what Comcast had publicly stated. Comcast repeated that it only slowed P2P traffic at times of congestion. Two Democratic members of the Senate committee, John Kerry and Byron Dorgan, proposed Congress should pass a law requiring net neutrality, which would clarify the FCC's authority to act in these cases. Republican members of the committee argued such a law could get in the way of innovation and prevent

PEER-TO-PEER NETWORKS

A peer-to-peer (P2P) network is a network of computers that allows certain files or folders to be shared among the network's users. In the early 2000s, P2P networks on the Internet were commonly used to share music. In 2006, more than 15 billion copyrighted songs were illegally shared or downloaded using P2P networks. In that same year, approximately 1 billion songs were sold legally on Apple's iTunes service.[4]

new business models from working. Martin himself said the FCC's four net neutrality principles allowed it to regulate on a case-by-case basis and that a law was not necessary.

The FCC met in August 2008 in response to the 2007 Vuze Inc. complaint. After taking additional testimony from both net neutrality proponents and opponents, it ruled against Comcast and ordered it to stop P2P interference on its network. The FCC ordered Comcast to come up with a new network management plan. If the company did not, the FCC warned Comcast it would be subject to further regulations. In response, Comcast said it was "considering all its legal options."[5]

BITTORRENT

BitTorrent is a system that allows for very fast downloading of large files, such as videos or movies. It works by breaking files up into many separate pieces, downloading those pieces from different sources on the network, then reassembling them. BitTorrent itself is legal, and the technology behind it has been described as innovative, but it can be used to download copyrighted material. It is up to users to police themselves.

COURT RULES IN FAVOR OF COMCAST

In September 2008, Comcast filed a lawsuit against the FCC's ruling. The next round in the battle for net neutrality had begun. The FCC had ruled against Comcast the previous month because P2P traffic throttling violated the net neutrality principles the FCC had adopted in 2005. Comcast countered that

Programmer Bram Cohen developed the BitTorrent system of sharing files in 2001.

the FCC's four principles were only statements of the agency's policy and not actual rules. Comcast went even further, saying the FCC lacked the legal authority to regulate broadband service at all.

COMCAST v. FCC
Comcast's 2010 victory over the FCC highlighted the FCC's problems in trying to regulate broadband services. Judge David Tatel ruled the FCC lacked the authority to regulate Comcast's activities. Gigi Sohn, president of the digital rights group Public Knowledge, said of the ruling: "Today's appeals court decision means there are no protections in the law for consumers' broadband services."[6] Thomas Lenard, president of the Technology Policy Institute, applauded the court's decision, saying net neutrality rules would hurt consumers. Again, the FCC's reluctance to classify broadband as a telecommunications service under common-carrier restrictions gave it little authority over broadband ISPs.

The US Court of Appeals for the District of Columbia Circuit sided with Comcast in 2010. It ruled the FCC lacked authority under the Telecommunications Act to regulate the network management practices of information service providers. Coincidentally, the ruling came at a time when Comcast was petitioning the FCC to approve its $30 billion merger with NBC Universal, the owners of a vast television and movie library. If the merger was permitted to go through, it would make Comcast a large content provider as well as an ISP.

FCC APPROVES NET NEUTRALITY REGULATIONS

As the US Court of Appeals was confirming the FCC had no legal basis for regulating broadband services, the FCC was taking testimony on a new set of net neutrality regulations. In December 2010, after more than seven years of heated debate, the FCC passed a compromise set of net neutrality rules governing broadband

The 2010 FCC net neutrality order contained three rules:

1. Transparency. Broadband Internet access providers were required to provide accurate information to both customers and content providers about their network management practices, performance, and cost.

2. No Blocking. Fixed broadband Internet access providers could not block customers from accessing any legal content, applications, or services. Mobile operators could not block lawful web pages or applications that competed against the operator's own voice or video services.

3. No Unreasonable Discrimination. A fixed broadband provider could not unreasonably discriminate in transmitting lawful Internet traffic over a customer's Internet broadband service.

services. The three new rules did not seem to please anyone. Net neutrality opponents said the rules would stifle broadband investment and innovation, whereas proponents said the rules did not go far enough and excluded the rapidly growing use of the Internet on mobile devices.

Not much changed with the adoption of the new rules. The four principles of net neutrality adopted as FCC policy in 2005 had now become three regulations. Republicans in the US House of Representatives passed resolutions meant to undo the FCC regulations, but they had little chance of getting the law passed by the Democratic Senate or signed by President Obama, who strongly supported net neutrality. Comcast, the largest US cable company, offered guarded support for the FCC regulations and agreed to comply as a condition of its merger with NBC Universal. Verizon filed a lawsuit the following month challenging the new rules. The battle continued.

Mergers between telecommunications companies are often targeted by protestors as potential threats to net neutrality.

CHAPTER 4

THE NET NEUTRALITY PENDULUM SWINGS

From 2013 to 2015, the status of net neutrality continued going back and forth. Decisions by the courts, businesses, and the FCC would all sway the debate in favor of ISPs. But public opinion and a presidential statement would help shift FCC rules back in favor of net neutrality.

THE VERIZON DECISION

Verizon called the FCC's 2010 net neutrality rules "excessive" and "arbitrary and capricious."[1] Verizon sued the FCC. The result was a mixed bag for the FCC. In *Verizon v. FCC*, the DC Circuit ruled the FCC could impose regulations on the network management practices of broadband providers. But it agreed with Verizon that this authority did not allow the FCC to impose common carriage restrictions on information services. The court upheld the commission's transparency rules but removed the blocking and unreasonable discrimination rules.

Vocal protesters strongly influenced the debate over net neutrality.

VERIZON v. FCC

After the FCC's 2010 ruling on net neutrality, Verizon complained the rules would have made it hard for it to manage growing network traffic. It wanted a "two-sided market" for companies that wanted to pay for faster service. Further, it argued that any effort by the government to keep it from making such deals went against its rights of free speech under the First Amendment.

On January 14, 2014, a federal appeals court ruled in favor of Verizon and against the FCC. In his majority opinion, Circuit Judge David Tatel said that although the FCC had the legal authority to regulate Verizon and other ISPs, in this case it had overreached. In its 2010 ruling, the FCC had classified broadband providers as not being common carriers, which meant the FCC could not treat them as such. Verizon executive Randal Milch said, "Today's decision will not change consumers' ability to access and use the Internet as they do now. The court's decision will allow more room for innovation."[3]

Following this court decision, net neutrality proponents worried ISPs would immediately take advantage of charging content providers for different tiers of high-speed service. If so, the Internet would no longer be an equal playing field. Reacting to the decision, former FCC commissioner Michael Copps said, "Without prompt corrective action by the commission to reclassify broadband [as a telecommunication service], this awful ruling will serve as a sorry memorial to the corporate [removal] of free speech."[2] With both the Comcast and Verizon court decisions, the FCC had twice failed to make its case that it could impose common carrier restrictions on information service providers.

THE COMCAST-NETFLIX PROBLEM

In the spring of 2013 and extending into 2014, millions of Americans shared a similar frustrating problem—some of their Internet services stopped working the way they should. Movies streaming on Netflix would not load, videoconferencing did not work, and gaming became almost impossible. The outages usually happened during the workday or evening, prime times for getting work done or relaxing.

Between October 2013 and November 2014, the speeds at which Comcast was delivering Netflix programming dropped 27 percent.[4] The cause appeared to be a dispute between Comcast and Cogent Communications, the company

THROTTLING AND BLOCKING

Because an ISP is the only pathway for Internet service into a home, it can control the content of what a person can access and when it can be accessed. An ISP can manipulate Internet access in a number of ways. It can block content to make it seem as though the website or service does not exist. It can deliberately slow down some content over others. Or it can allow periods of widespread congestion over its network and slow down everything. A 2014 report by Measurement Lab Research Consortium showed that customers of all major US ISPs had slowdowns once their traffic passed the boundary from the networks of popular content providers. Many net neutrality opponents allege ISPs manipulated content delivery in 2013 and 2014 in an attempt to negotiate speed-for-fee rate hikes with content providers such as Netflix.

The popular video streaming service Netflix found itself at the center of a dispute about Internet regulations in 2014.

Netflix paid to deliver its content over the Internet to consumers. Netflix resolved the dispute by signing a direct interconnection agreement with Comcast, similar to those that other content providers such as Apple, Google, Facebook, and Microsoft had signed. Importantly, these interconnection agreements did not involve paid prioritization over the Comcast network, and therefore they did not violate net neutrality. Comcast had been bound to net neutrality even after the *Verizon* decision, as a condition of the FCC's approval of its acquisition of NBC Universal. Nonetheless, as soon as Netflix signed the deal, streaming speed and quality of Netflix content to Comcast customers improved, which further fanned the flames of the controversy in favor of greater FCC oversight of Internet providers.

Before making its agreement with Comcast, Netflix repeatedly complained to the FCC, accusing Comcast and Verizon of using throttling and blocking practices. The FCC added the complaints to its growing list of net neutrality concerns. Regarding the Netflix situation, FCC chairman Tom Wheeler said, "Consumers must get what they pay for. As the consumer's representative we need to know what is going on."[5] However, he considered this an issue between businesses, rather than between businesses and consumers. He leaned toward not regulating the Internet. Verizon and Comcast agreed with him. A Verizon spokesperson said in an interview regarding Netflix, "Internet traffic exchange has always been handled through commercial agreements."[6]

MORE CONTROVERSY CHANGES A RULING

In April 2014, Wheeler announced the FCC was considering a proposal that would impose net neutrality restrictions on ISPs. Consistent with the DC Circuit's guidance in *Verizon*, however, the proposal would allow ISPs to offer fast lanes to content providers. But a series of events would ultimately change his mind and lead to stricter regulation. In May, a coalition of more than 100 tech companies—including Google and Microsoft—said the proposed fast-lane rules were "a grave threat to the Internet."[7]

In June, John Oliver aired his *Last Week Tonight* segment, and the FCC was subsequently flooded with public demands for net neutrality. In mid-July, Google, Facebook, Twitter, Amazon.com, Yahoo, LinkedIn, Reddit, Yelp, Expedia, and other content providers sent a document to the FCC throwing their support behind net neutrality and urging the FCC to protect the open Internet. Although those against government regulation of ISPs also made their voices heard, including Republicans in Congress and several big tech companies, the balance seemed to be shifting in favor of net neutrality.

Then, in August and October, President Obama came out fully in favor of net neutrality, and in November he issued a written statement asking for strong net neutrality rules and clear authority to implement them. He urged Wheeler to end the era of "light touch," and he appealed for more oversight and transparency of ISPs. Specifically, he proposed Internet access now be reclassified as a utility under Title II of the Telecommunications Act—the same classification applied to telephone companies. This would subject the Internet to new regulations to preserve net neutrality.

> "An open Internet is essential to the American economy, and increasingly to our very way of life. . . . The time has come for the FCC to recognize that broadband service is of the same importance and must carry the same obligations as so many of the other vital services do. "[8]
>
> —President Barack Obama, in a November 10, 2014, statement

Even before becoming president, Obama expressed support for net neutrality in a meeting with Google CEO Eric Schmidt.

In January 2015, Wheeler hinted at a Title II reclassification. This worried Republicans in Congress—including Senator John Thune and Representative Fred Upton—who were against reclassification. They quickly drafted a bill favorable to ISPs. Though they would eventually drop the legislation for lack of support, their attempt spurred Wheeler to push the FCC for an early vote.

THE 2015 FCC RULING

On February 26, 2015, in a 3-to-2 vote along political party lines, the FCC approved new rules requiring ISPs to act in the public interest when providing Internet connections. It banned ISPs from slowing or blocking Web traffic or creating paid fast lanes on the Internet. The ruling also gave the Internet common-carrier status, making it officially a telecommunications service rather than an information service. ISPs were now subject to the same regulations as telephone companies.

With the ruling, the FCC hoped to get rid of the legal vagueness from its earlier 2005 and 2010 rulings. It hoped courts would now be less likely to rule against it, as had happened repeatedly in the past. The FCC could now also fine ISPs if regulators found companies were using unreasonable business practices. Some sections of Title II would not apply with this ruling. For example, the FCC would not set price caps, as it did with telephone lines. This meant the rates ISPs charged consumers for Internet access would not need prior approval, although the FCC could investigate consumer complaints of unfair pricing.

SWIFT REACTION

Reactions to the ruling came quickly from both sides of the net neutrality issue. Republican FCC commissioners Mike O'Rielly and Ajit Pai, who voted against the plan, asserted that President Obama had unfairly used his influence to get the plan passed. They called the ruling a "half-baked, illogical, internally inconsistent and indefensible document."[9] Republicans in Congress said the ruling was an example of government overreach into private enterprise. They worried it would discourage investment and drive up consumer costs and taxes.

THE MOBILE ISSUE

In 2010, US policymakers chose to treat Internet connections that went to mobile phones differently from the connections that went to homes and offices. At the time, few people were using their cell phones to connect to the Internet, and the FCC believed mobile networks were growing and had healthy competition. As a result, they gave mobile carriers an exemption from many net neutrality requirements. But as time went on, the lines between mobile and home connections began to blur as people connected to the Internet wherever they went. In its February 2015 decision, the FCC decided—for the first time—to apply net neutrality protections to wireless services for smartphones and tablets.

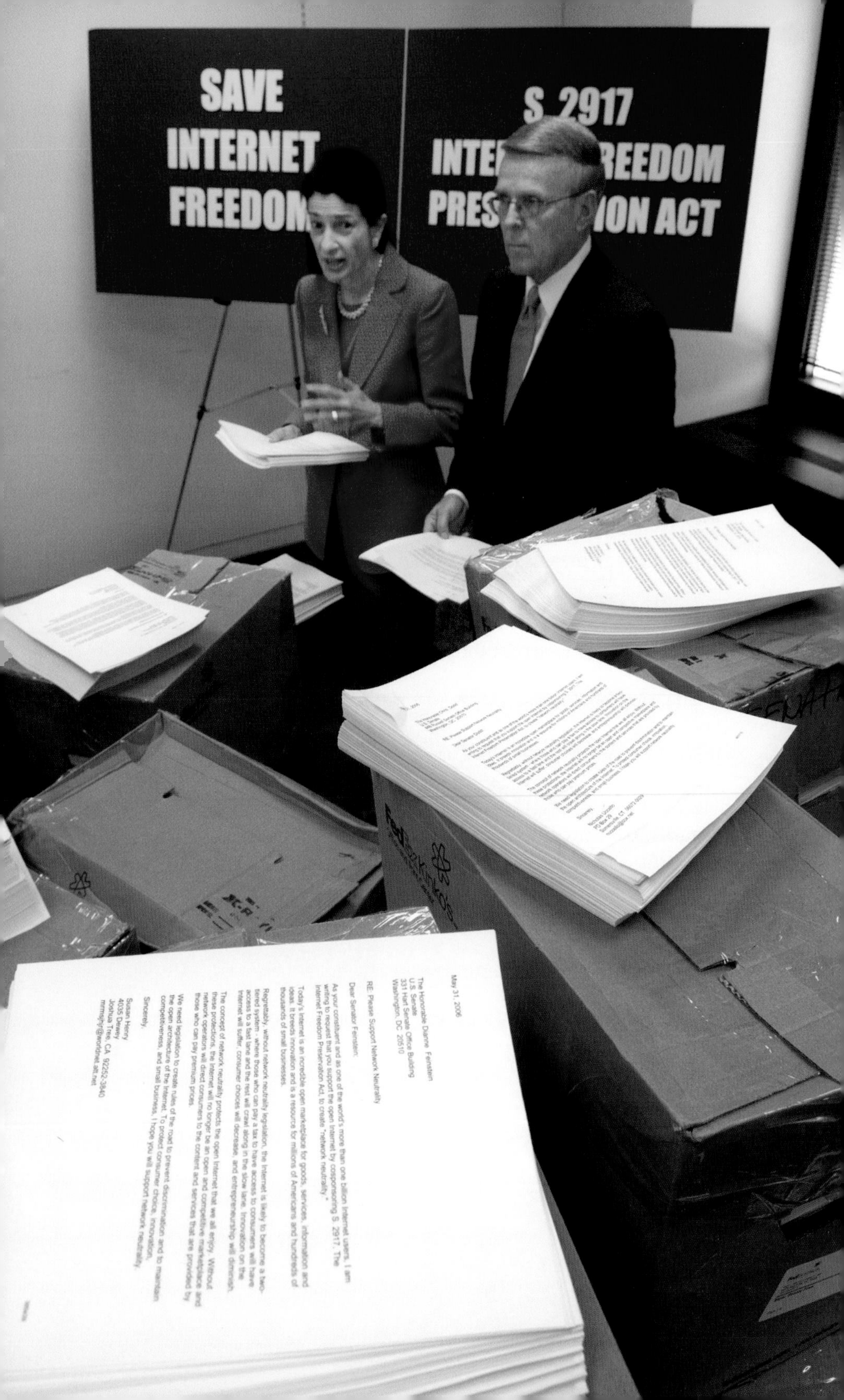
SAVE
INTERNET
FREEDOM
S 2917

In a process called "peering connections," content providers bypass the Internet backbone and directly connect to ISPs. By 2015, the largest Internet content providers, including Google, Facebook, and Netflix, were all using such connections. Although the process allows for improved speeds and gives big content providers an advantage over smaller providers that cannot afford such agreements, they were not included in the 2015 net neutrality decision. The FCC does not regulate peering connections, though it has indicated it may do so in the future.

On the other side of the issue, FCC chairman Wheeler said the Internet was "too important to let broadband providers be the ones making the rules."[10] Michael Beckerman, president of the Internet Association, which includes online companies Google, Facebook, and others, said the FCC vote was "a welcome step in our effort to create strong, enforceable net neutrality rules."[11] Lawsuits were expected to come quickly, and they did. The FCC's new net neutrality rules went into effect on June 12, 2015, but it was unclear how long they would last.

Senators Olympia Snowe, *left*, and Byron Dorgan pose with stacks of 175,000 letters of public support for net neutrality.

CHAPTER 5

NET NEUTRALITY SUPPORTERS

The fight for net neutrality has resulted in a strange partnership between groups often at odds with each other. On this issue, consumer and human rights advocates are aligned with some big businesses—they all want a free and open Internet with equal access for all. But the primary concerns of these groups are not always the same. Content providers do not want to be charged for different tiers of high-speed service. Their battles with ISPs on this issue are well documented in the news media and court cases. The concerns of consumer and human rights advocates, on the other hand, are not quite as well documented. These net neutrality proponents point to a number of reasons why they believe government regulation is necessary when a few ISPs have too much control.

Supporters of net neutrality have put pressure on government officials to enforce net neutrality.

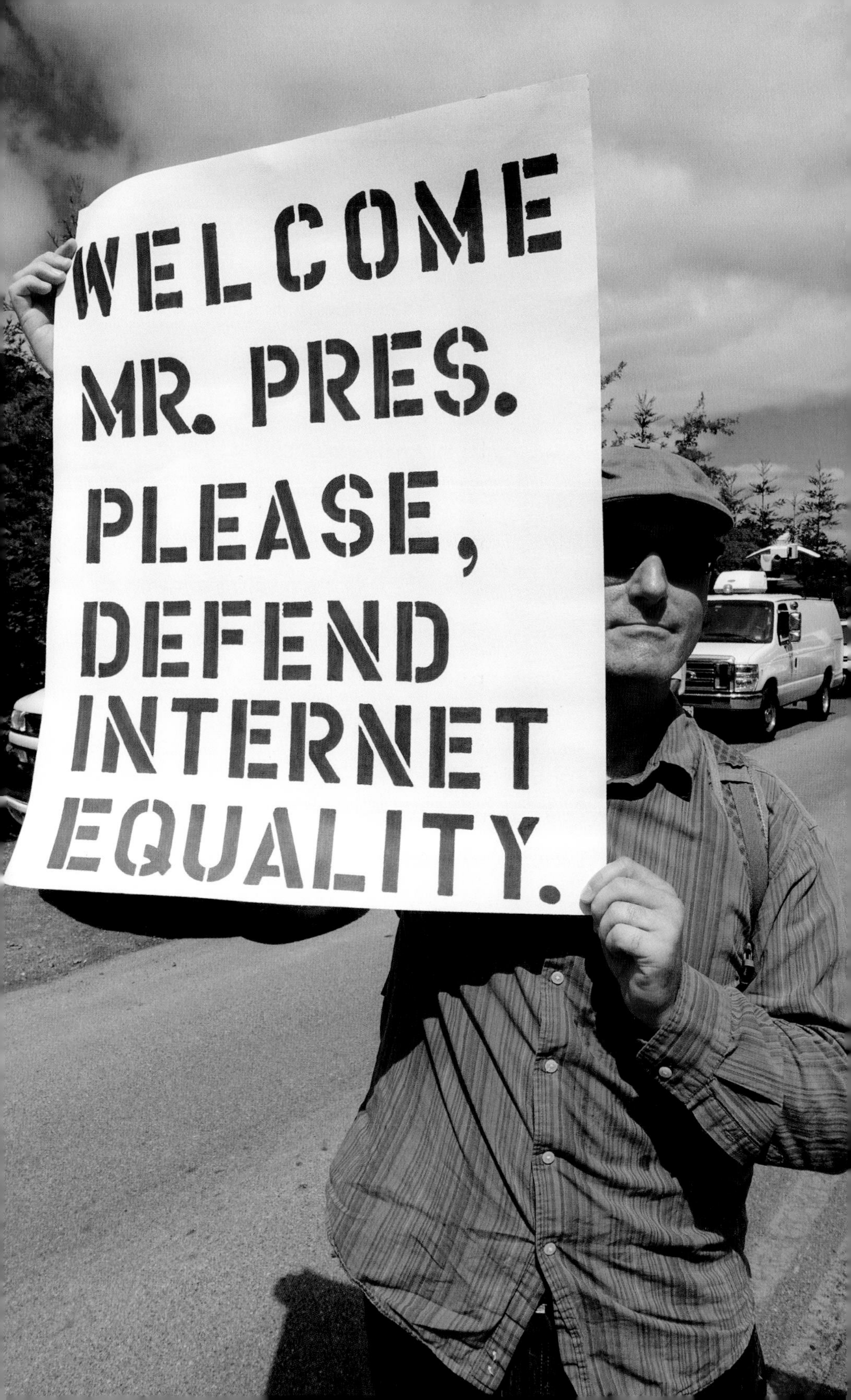
WELCOME
MR. PRES.
PLEASE,
DEFEND
INTERNET
EQUALITY.

VIRTUAL MONOPOLIES

Net neutrality experts accuse a few ISPs of having complete or nearly complete control of Internet services in many areas of the United States. If a consumer wants to change Internet providers, he or she has few or no alternate options in many areas. A Center for Public Integrity study showed most US residents had access to Internet service from no more than two companies. This compared unfavorably to the situation in other countries, such as France, where consumers can typically choose between seven ISPs.

The same study found telecommunications companies appeared to split US territory amongst them to limit competition. For example, although there appeared to be a choice of three ISPs in Seattle, Washington, in reality a single large ISP—Comcast— provided 95 percent of the Internet service to the area. Internet service maps of other major US cities showed a similar pattern, and the same was true for DSL services.[2]

Studies of the US broadband market tend to bear out the idea that costs rise and service suffers with a lack of competition. A 2013 study conducted by Ookla, a company that tests Internet download speed, showed that US Internet speed was slower than that in 30 other countries, including the Czech Republic and Estonia.[3] In a May 2014 national survey conducted by the American Customer Satisfaction Index (ACSI), Comcast and Time Warner Cable's Internet service businesses had the lowest customer satisfaction ratings of all ISPs in the United States. In fact, these two companies came in dead last for customer satisfaction among all companies that ASCI rates, including airlines, banks, health insurance companies, and utilities. In 2014, the average US customer paid more than twice what customers paid in parts of Europe and Asia for 25-megabit connections.[4] More than 8 percent of US households said they could not afford broadband at all.[5]

INTERNET SLOWDOWN

Some net neutrality proponents say ISPs have no interest in increasing bandwidth because it is too expensive and there is not enough competition to make ISPs want to change. In 2014, Mark Taylor, vice president of backbone provider Level 3, found evidence five ISPs in the United States were refusing to upgrade their infrastructure.

Many net neutrality experts see a relationship between ISPs and electricity wholesalers, companies that provide electric power to retail electricity companies. As an example, they point to the late 1990s, when California deregulated its electric utilities. At the time, state officials thought a free-market business model—one with little government regulation—would make power companies more efficient and bring down prices. But the opposite happened. Wholesale electricity suppliers, such as Enron, shut down power plants to make supply seem low. As a result, energy prices rose 800 percent and the state had brownouts and blackouts.[7]

Net neutrality proponents assert that, like Enron, ISPs have an incentive to starve the market to set higher fees. And they do this by not building infrastructure that would make bandwidth cheaper or the Internet faster. Experts argue gigabit-per-second (Gbps) broadband could easily become a reality. A gigabit per second is equal to 1,000 megabits per second (Mbps). In 2013, Comcast showed off a 3-Gbps system at a trade show.[8] But in March 2015, the fastest speed delivered by Comcast during primetime viewing hours was only 3.3 Mbps.[9] Most customers pay for 25 Mbps or less. Blair Levin, a former FCC official, said in an interview, "Is there anywhere else in the ecosystem where somebody demonstrates something that's really cool and great, and faster and better, and doesn't put it out for more than two years?"[10] ISPs argue they have not increased bandwidth because of supply and demand. They say customers are happy with the speeds they have and are not asking for more.

VERTICAL INTEGRATION

Making this situation even worse, say some net neutrality experts, is a practice called vertical integration. Vertical integration happens when a company expands into another business closely related to something the company already produces. One example of this is when AT&T made telephone hardware. It is not necessarily a bad thing, as it can help companies decrease costs and increase efficiency. But it is another matter when a company has a monopoly or near monopoly.

In 2011, Comcast purchased NBC Universal, a content provider that owned NBC broadcast stations, the Internet streaming service Hulu, and cable channels, including Bravo, USA, and E!. As part of the Comcast-NBC merger, the FCC required Comcast not interfere in Hulu's operations or use discriminatory pricing with its competitors. But net neutrality proponents worried that as both a service provider and a content provider, Comcast would favor its own content over that of others. Free Press wrote in a November 2009 report, "Comcast/NBC will have an incentive to prioritize NBC shows over other local and independent voices and programs."[11] In April 2015, FCC and Department of Justice investigations found Comcast had failed to adhere to several of its required conditions, including not interfering with Hulu's management. The FCC fined Comcast $800,000 for its misbehavior, which one publication called an "inconsequential sum" for such a large corporation.[12]

Comcast CEO Brian Roberts testifies before Congress about his company's planned merger with NBC Universal.

DANGER TO FREE SPEECH

A worst-case scenario some net neutrality proponents fear is that without regulation of ISPs, the Internet risks becoming like cable television, where the service provider also determines the content. For example, an ISP could charge content providers a large fee for customers to be able to view their websites. In this situation, customers might have access to a big news organization like *USA*

Today, which could easily afford the fee, but customers would be blocked from seeing a small news blog that could not afford the fee.

Likewise, an ISP might limit content based on its management's political, religious, or personal views. This scenario especially worries freedom-of-speech proponents, as more and more people get their news from the Internet. They argue that with the growth of the web as a source of news, equal access to different voices is critical to the democratic process.

GROWTH OF INTERNET NEWS

A poll conducted by the Pew Research Center in 2013 found 50 percent of Americans used the Internet as their main source of news. This percentage was below television (at 69 percent) but well above radio broadcasts (at 23 percent) and newspapers (at 28 percent). Among Americans between the ages of 18 and 29, 71 percent said the Internet was their main news source.[13]

BIG-MONEY POLITICS

Another complaint of net neutrality proponents is the relationship between ISPs and the government. They wonder how policies beneficial to consumers can ever win when broadband companies spend millions of dollars on lobbying every year and their CEOs are close to elected officials. During his eight years in office, President Obama regularly played golf with the CEO of Comcast.

Before the FCC made its 2015 ruling, more than 85 musicians and bands signed a letter encouraging FCC Chairman Tom Wheeler to support net neutrality regulations. The letter urged Wheeler to not give in to pressure from political opposition and big corporations, because musicians' livelihoods were at stake. Performers did not want ISPs blocking or discriminating against their online content because the ISP held a different political view or business preference. "Without clear and enforceable rules that let us compete alongside the biggest companies," the letter stated, "our ability to create and innovate will be threatened, if not extinguished. . . . Artists have endured tremendous consolidation in the media marketplace that has limited opportunities for many to reach audiences and earn a living."[16]

In May 2013, President Obama chose Tom Wheeler to be chairman of the FCC. Wheeler was a former lobbyist for telecom and cable companies. During the FCC's 2014–2015 net neutrality policy discussions, activists did not trust the FCC could make consumer friendly decisions when its chairman still had close ties to the companies that would benefit from his decisions.

ISPs spend a tremendous amount of money on lobbying members of Congress. In 2013, Comcast spent $18.8 million on lobbying.[14] The company ranked high compared to other corporations by this measure, coming in second only to defense contractor Northrop Grumman. Quid, a data analysis firm, found that as of September 2014, Verizon had spent $100 million lobbying the US Congress since 2009.[15]

With this kind of political influence, net neutrality proponents believe the cards will always be unfairly stacked against them. But those on the other side of the issue argue there is nothing wrong with lobbying or trying to make a profit. The US economy, they say, does best when government stays out of business' way.

LOBBYING

Lobbyists are paid by companies, industries, groups, and organizations to try to persuade US senators and representatives to change laws or create new laws that help the lobbyist's employer. Lobbyists have to register with the government and must follow certain guidelines, but they have long been considered a corrupting influence. The bad reputation stems from the idea that the people with the most money have the most influence. As early as 1869, a journalist wrote, "Winding in and out through the long, devious basement passage, crawling through the corridors, trailing its slimy length from gallery to committee room, at last it lies stretched at full length on the floor of Congress—this dazzling reptile, this huge, scaly serpent of the lobby."[17] Lobbying is protected under the First Amendment, and many busy members of Congress appreciate the information lobbyists share with them on complex issues.

President Obama played golf with Comcast CEO Brian Roberts in August 2013. Many people criticize the close relationship between political and corporate leaders.

CHAPTER 6

OPPOSITION TO NET NEUTRALITY

Interestingly, people on both sides of the net neutrality issue say they are in favor of an open Internet. The dispute is whether—and how much—government regulation is needed to preserve it. Generally, those against regulation include large ISPs and Republican and Libertarian politicians, who tend to oppose government restrictions on business.

ARGUMENTS AGAINST REGULATION

The range of arguments against government involvement in the Internet boils down to two basic beliefs: that regulation deters investment and that the FCC has no right to upend the hands-off Internet policy it has had since the mid-1990s.

"For most of the Internet era . . . tech policy has been a bright spot in Washington. Not only has it been a rare example of bipartisanship, but also of regulatory wisdom."[1] This statement from Larry Downes, author and project director of the Georgetown

Republican senator Ted Cruz described net neutrality as a threat to the Internet.

USTELECOM ASSOCIATION ET AL. V. FCC

Shortly after the FCC's February 2015 net neutrality decision that classified the Internet as a utility similar to telephone service, groups representing the broadband industry filed suit to reverse the ruling. The groups included USTelecom Association, the National Cable & Telecommunications Association, CTIA-The Wireless Association, the American Cable Association, the Wireless Internet Service Providers Association, AT&T, and CenturyLink. In July 2015, they discussed four problems with the FCC ruling. First, they said the FCC had no right to reverse years of nonregulation. Second, they said it was illegal because Congress classified the Internet as an information service. Third, they said it distorted the meaning of the Telecommunications Act. Finally, they said the decision-making process before the ruling was not carried out properly. "[The ruling] is, in short, a sweeping bureaucratic power grab by a self-appointed 'Department of the Internet,'" the group wrote in its court brief.[2] In turn, the FCC argued against each of these points. Its main argument was that the Telecommunications Act was ambiguous, and because the FCC was the expert on telecommunications services, it—not the courts—should be allowed to interpret the act.

Center for Business and Public Policy, sums up what many people believe was a terrible mistake made by the FCC with its 2015 net neutrality ruling. He and others against government regulation of the Internet argue that up until 2015, the US federal government had interfered very little with the workings of the Internet. This was partly by choice, and partly because whatever regulations the FCC did enact were struck down by federal appeals courts. The Internet had worked just fine without regulations, so why, they argued, should the government change a system that was not broken?

People against net neutrality regulations point to the success of the Internet to support their claims that no government interference is necessary. According to the National Cable & Telecommunications Association, a cable-lobbying group, ISPs have built the world's leading cable, mobile, and fiber networks, investing more than $1 trillion in new infrastructure since the 1990s. The association adds that broadband reaches 99 percent of Americans and 100 Mbps connections are available in 85 percent of homes.[3] Net neutrality opponents also argue fast lanes are at times appropriate and even necessary. An example would be the use of an Internet connection to provide medical services, where an interruption or slowdown could prove harmful to patients. A ban on paid prioritization could also chill investment in such applications.

TREATING THE INTERNET AS A UTILITY

Prior to the FCC's 2015 net neutrality decision, which gave the FCC regulatory power over ISPs, those against net neutrality regulations argued imposing century-old telephone-utility regulations would choke growth and investment. Former FCC chairman Michael Powell wrote in an editorial, "Network investment would suffer, and the push to reach more households would slow."[4] He asserted that bureaucratic oversight would slow innovation. Further, he said heavily regulated utilities tended to be slow, inefficient, and sometimes even corrupt. He and others argued the Internet should not be forced down the same road.

COMCAST/ TIME WARNER MERGER

In February 2014, Comcast, the United States' largest cable provider, announced it intended to buy Time Warner, the nation's second-largest cable company. Due to drawn-out investigations by the FCC and a skeptical Department of Justice, it appeared the merger would not go through. Comcast pulled out of the deal in April 2015. In a statement, the Department of Justice said it had "significant concerns that the merger would make Comcast an unavoidable gatekeeper for the Internet-based services that rely on broadband connection to reach consumers."[5] Consumer rights and other advocacy groups had similar concerns. The merger would have given Comcast control of approximately half of the US broadband market. Even with the 2015 FCC net neutrality rules in effect, the combined companies would have been very powerful in fighting those rules and influencing the broadband market.

For their parts, both Comcast and Time Warner said the merger would not reduce competition, because they did not

Protesters spoke out strongly against the proposed merger between Comcast and Time Warner.

compete in the same markets. They claimed their combined resources would improve customer service. But regulators did not buy this argument, and neither did the public, which submitted more than 800,000 individual comments to the FCC about the merger. "Mergers in service industries usually result in lower customer satisfaction, at least in the short term," said David VanAmburg, director of the ACSI. "It's hard to see how combining two negatives will be a positive for consumers."[6] Even though the deal collapsed, future mergers in the broadband industry might still lie ahead.

Other companies besides ISPs agreed with this assessment. In December 2014, prior to the FCC's 2015 ruling, 60 technology companies, including IBM and Cisco, signed a letter arguing against treating the Internet as a utility. The letter stated, in part, "Title II is going to lead to a slowdown, if not a hold, in broadband build out, because if you don't know that you can recover on your investment, you won't make it."[7] In the letter, the companies implied the end result of the regulation could be another recession, or even a depression. Even some content providers that support net neutrality are concerned Title II regulations might hinder innovation and investment.

PRIVACY, TAXES, AND GEOGRAPHY

In June 2013, Edward Snowden, a contractor working for the National Security Agency (NSA), released hundreds of top-secret

Snowden's privacy revelations drew attention to government oversight of the Internet.

documents to journalists. The documents revealed secret government programs were gathering data on the Internet activity of average Americans. At least one of these programs tampered with US-made computer routing devices. With the FCC's new regulations, anti-interventionists said the government would have to monitor telecom and cable companies' broadband connections. "Don't be surprised if that means the government needs to be able to install its own hardware and software at critical points to monitor Internet traffic," warned Internet entrepreneur Joshua Steimle in *Forbes* magazine. "Once installed, can we trust this government, or any government, to use that access in a benign manner?"[8]

Antiregulators insisted taxes would go up as a result of the 2015 FCC ruling. Republican FCC commissioner Ajit Pai said in an interview immediately after the ruling was announced: "More Internet taxes are coming. It's just a matter of when."[9] Taxes could not rise right away

REPUBLICANS TAKE ACTION

Republicans in Congress failed to pass legislation prior to the FCC's 2015 net neutrality ruling, but they revisited the issue in the summer of 2015. This time, they attached a policy rider, a provision added to a bill that often has nothing to do with the bill itself, to a spending bill. The rider would have blocked the FCC from implementing net neutrality rules. The rider also would have prevented the FCC from setting rates for Internet access. As of November 2015, Senate Commerce Committee Chairman John Thune doubted the net neutrality rider would make it into the final spending bill, because "it would be so controversial."[10]

because the Internet Tax Freedom Act banned taxes on Internet access. But once the Internet was deemed a telephone-like utility in 2015, nothing was preventing states from pushing Congress to allow them to tax consumers for Internet access the same way they taxed for telephone service.

> One way or another, I am committed to moving a legislative solution, preferably bipartisan, to stop monopoly-era phone regulations that harm Internet consumers and innovation. [11]
>
> —John Thune, Republican US Senator from South Dakota

As evidence that big ISPs provide poor service, proponents of net neutrality point to the fact that broadband speeds in the US are much slower than in many other countries. Antiregulators counter a lack of speed is due to America's geography. Due to the nation's size and spread-out population centers, broadband has not reached all parts of the United States, which means far-flung areas are still using dial-up service. They say comparing Internet connectivity in the vast United States with connectivity in much smaller countries, such as Estonia and South Korea, skews reality.

ANGER SPURS LEGAL ACTION

After the February 2015 FCC net neutrality ruling, ISPs feared they would also become subject to price controls. A consortium of ISPs, including AT&T and Verizon, sued the government in March 2015. They tried to overturn the FCC's new rules, asserting the regulations were "arbitrary, capricious, and an abuse of

Net neutrality protests often focus on the slow speeds that could result from the absence of net neutrality.

discretion."[12] That same month in Texas, a small ISP called Alamo Broadband filed a similar lawsuit.

In June 2015, a circuit court rejected the consortium's attempt to keep the net neutrality rules from going into effect until the court hears its challenge. A fuller hearing was held in December 2015. Analysts expected a decision would come in 2016. It was clear the battle over net neutrality was far from over.

CHAPTER 7

NET NEUTRALITY WORLDWIDE

As the United States grapples with the issue of net neutrality, so does the rest of the world. At the United Nations 2014 Internet Governance Forum, no consensus could be reached on who controls the Internet or even how to define net neutrality. In developed countries, the net neutrality battle is often over the balance between free enterprise and government regulation. In less-developed countries, the battle is often over control of information. As use of the Internet continues expanding throughout the world, the question of net neutrality takes on added importance.

GLOBAL INTERNET ACCESS

According to a United Nations Broadband Commission (UNBC) report, approximately 3.2 billion people, or 43 percent of the world's population, had regular access to the Internet in 2015.[1] The ten countries with the greatest percentage of their populations

In the absence of net neutrality efforts from the United Nations, each of the world's countries takes its own approach to the issue.

FASTEST AND CHEAPEST INTERNET

A 2014 survey conducted by Akamai Technologies ranked the United States seventeenth in the world in average broadband connection speed. From fastest to slowest, the top ten countries in the survey were South Korea, Hong Kong, Japan, Sweden, Switzerland, the Netherlands, Latvia, Ireland, Czech Republic, and Finland. South Korea averaged 22.2 Mbps, whereas the United States averaged 11.4 Mbps.[4]

The US public also paid more for Internet service than people paid in many other countries. A 2015 report by the Center for Public Integrity compared what consumers paid in five US cities with what consumers paid in five French cities. US prices were as much as 3.5 times higher than prices in France for similar service.[5] Customers in the United States could also expect to pay more than twice for 25 Mbps what a customer paid for 25 Mbps in parts of Europe and Asia. In Hong Kong, China, or Seoul, South Korea, $50 went ten times further than in Washington, DC.[6]

using the Internet were all located in Europe. Approximately 4.2 billion people were without regular Internet access, many of them in sub-Saharan Africa.[2] The same UNBC report urged countries to do everything they could to make broadband services affordable and accessible. According to the report, "It is increasingly vital to extend access to digital education services, new capabilities, culture, entertainment, healthcare, financial and commercial services, along with training and education."[3]

Even with these sizable gaps in broadband access, international spending on telecom services was expected to reach $3.8 trillion in 2015, up from $1.67 trillion spent in 2013. Access to the Internet via mobile broadband was also widespread. The International Telecommunications Union projected that by 2019,

6.5 billion mobile phones would be broadband-connected.[7] Mobile broadband services are especially suited to developing countries and isolated rural areas, because they rely less on costly and difficult-to-install cables or fiber optics. With Internet access expanding, countries are increasingly faced with issues of net neutrality and open access.

GLOBAL NET NEUTRALITY RULES AND LAWS

In 2015, the United States became the fifth country to pass net neutrality rules to limit Internet fast lanes and keep ISPs from favoring some content providers over others. In 2009, the Canadian Radio-television and Telecommunications Commission had passed net neutrality rules requiring Canadian ISPs to treat Internet content equally. In 2010, Chile had become the first country to pass net neutrality legislation—not only rules—with its General Telecommunications Law. In 2011, the Dutch government adopted net neutrality, with rules banning mobile phone operators from blocking or charging consumers extra for using Internet-based services. In 2014, Brazil passed a strong net neutrality law that banned ISPs from charging content providers higher rates for high-bandwidth content, such as streamed movies. It also placed limits on the amount of consumer data websites such as Facebook and Google could store about Brazilian citizens.

Like their counterparts in the United States, Indian activists spoke out for net neutrality in 2015.

In June 2015, after two years of fierce debate, the European Union (EU) agreed to the text of a telecommunications law promoting equal treatment of Internet traffic beginning in 2016. The EU Parliament passed the law in October 2015. The legislation is less restrictive than the rules passed by the FCC in 2015 in the United States and allows ISPs to charge extra for some "innovative services," such as video conferencing or video surgery. Blocking and throttling will also be allowed under certain situations. For example, they might be used to prevent or slow a cyberattack or during times of high Internet traffic.

India's regulators debated passing fast-lane legislation in 2015, as well as giving ISPs permission to charge consumers extra for using services such as YouTube and Skype. Net neutrality advocates in India argued these rules would cost consumers too much money and keep smaller Internet businesses from being competitive. Indian Internet activists organized campaigns to change the final rules.

> **"** One of the main reasons the Internet has been so successful is that people have generally been able to use it how they wish. The worst thing [international] policy makers could do to the network would be to allow telecom companies to mess with that. **"** [9]
>
> —Editorial Board, *New York Times*, April 2015

FREEDOM ON THE NET

Equal access to the Internet is a hallmark of net neutrality, and it varies widely from one country to another. Freedom House, an independent watchdog organization founded in 1941, is "dedicated to the expansion of freedom and democracy around the world."[8] Since 2011, the organization has produced a yearly "Freedom on the Net" report, which analyzes Internet access and digital media around the world. The 2014 report sorted 65 countries into three categories: free, partly free, and not free. The top three free countries were Iceland, Estonia, and Canada, with the United States coming in at number six. The top three partly free countries were Nigeria, South Korea, and Ukraine. The bottom three not free countries were China, Syria, and Iran.

The report also documented a continuing decline in Internet freedom during four consecutive years, from 2011 through 2014. During that time, governments that used to be more secretive about controlling the Internet were now passing laws legalizing repression and criminalizing online dissent. Forty-one countries passed or proposed legislation that penalized legitimate online speech, increased government control of Internet content, and expanded government surveillance. As a result, more people were being detained or prosecuted for their online activities. Thirty-eight countries arrested citizens for their communications regarding social and political issues. Journalists were also affected. Independent news websites were coming under more pressure from countries to repress reporting of internal

FREEDOM SCORE CRITERIA

The international watchdog organization Freedom House bases its Internet freedom scores on three criteria. The first is obstacles to Internet access. The second is limits on content due to filtering, blocking, and censorship. The third is violations of users' rights, including privacy and protections from harassment or physical attacks.

Large Internet companies, such as Google, have enormous data storage centers in countries around the world.

conflicts. In Syria, Egypt, Turkey, and Ukraine, for example, dozens of citizen journalists were attacked while reporting on antigovernment demonstrations.

In a practice called data localization, some governments began requiring foreign Web companies—such as Google and Facebook—to build data storage centers within their countries' borders. These requirements were expensive and a roadblock for smaller Web companies wanting to operate in these countries. It also meant information on individual consumers could be exposed to the prying eyes of local law enforcement. Between July 2013 and July 2014, both Russia and Vietnam passed laws requiring web companies to have at least one data-collection server located within their borders.

The 2014 Freedom of the Net report found two additional threats placing the rights, and even lives, of Internet users at risk. One was the rising harassment of women and lesbian, gay, bisexual, transgender, and intersex (LGBTI) people. Women and members of the LGBTI community had been harassed, threatened, and attacked violently as a result of their online activities. In Pakistan in 2013, a woman was stoned to death after a tribal court convicted her of possessing a mobile phone. In that same year, the Russian parliament passed a law against LGBTI "propaganda." Vigilante groups then used online tools to lure gay men to meet in person, then physically beat them and threatened them with public exposure.

The report found another threat to Internet freedom was a lack of online security for human rights activists and people with political views opposing those of the ruling

In 2013, NSA contractor Edward Snowden released thousands of documents revealing large-scale data collection and storage programs conducted by the NSA on foreign citizens. Brazilian net neutrality legislation had stalled until that point, but it became an issue again when the NSA revelations alerted the Brazilian public to the safety of their personal data. In 2014, Brazilian legislators passed the Marco Civil da Internet law. The highly regarded Brazilian law included strong privacy provisions, strong protection for online freedom of expression, and no traffic discrimination. The law was considered a positive example for other countries. It even gained praise from Tim Berners-Lee, the man credited with inventing the World Wide Web, who said the legislation was effective in balancing the rights and duties of governments, corporations, and users.

government. In 2013, a computer virus attack targeted members of an Ethiopian exile community, including the opposition figure Tadesse Kersmo and the staff of the US-based news agency ESAT. The attacks were traced back to people working with the Ethiopian government. Even with these infringements on Internet freedoms, ordinary citizens have pushed back against restraints, demanding more Internet protections for themselves and others. In some cases, as in Brazil, the public outcry has led to effective net neutrality legislation.

CHAPTER 8

THE FUTURE OF NET NEUTRALITY

The future of net neutrality is uncertain. In the United States, strong regulations passed by the FCC in 2015 could be affected by court cases, congressional legislation, and even presidential elections. Some net neutrality proponents wonder whether locally run networks are a solution. Globally, some countries have strong net neutrality laws. Other nations simply want to access the Internet any way they can.

MUNICIPAL NETWORKS

Net neutrality advocates have long argued that the United States' few giant ISPs are not acting in the public's interest. They say that due to a lack of competition, ISPs charge high prices and provide poor service. Starting in the early 2000s, some communities began creating their own municipal networks, offering fast and inexpensive fiber-optic broadband connections to local citizens. Experts who study community-owned networks have claimed

Under the leadership of chairman Tom Wheeler, the FCC made moves in favor of net neutrality in 2015.

Kutztown, Pennsylvania, is one of many US communities that has moved ahead with a municipal broadband network.

municipal networks are generally more reliable, faster, and cheaper, and also provide better service than big ISPs do. Some claim this is the future of broadband. Supporters also describe municipal networks as a way to limit negative tactics used by big ISPs, such as fast lanes and data slowing.

But there are downsides. Municipal networks are expensive to build and maintain, and they are not always financially successful. Rural residents may be left out if connecting them to networks is too costly. Once a government picks an Internet delivery system, it is stuck with that system in the event technology changes. And private ISPs can have an unfair disadvantage competing against government-funded ISPs. Municipal networks have faced many legal hurdles from state governments, especially when networks have tried to expand their services into other areas. For example, in 2014, two local governments in Wilson, North Carolina, and Chattanooga, Tennessee, filed petitions with the FCC to override state laws that were keeping them from sharing their fast and cheap Internet services with neighboring towns.

In a separate ruling, the FCC took municipal ISPs into consideration on the same day as its 2015 net neutrality ruling. At the time, 19 states restricted towns and cities from creating their own broadband networks. Many of these state laws were backed by cable and phone companies. The FCC's ruling preempted state laws, allowing public ISPs to expand as they wished. But whether municipal networks would become the ISPs of the future remained to be seen. Like other aspects of the FCC's net neutrality ruling, public networks face more legal battles. And detractors, including state lawmakers, worried that if a municipal ISP failed, state taxpayers would have to bear the costs.

LEGISLATION AND POLICY CHANGES

The shape of net neutrality in the United States could change once again if the FCC's 2015 ruling were overturned in the courts. Congressional legislation might also strengthen or derail net neutrality. Congressional hearings began in March 2015 with hopes for a bipartisan solution. Republicans wanted to remove ISPs from Title II common-carrier status, and Democrats wanted to keep the net neutrality provisions of no blocking, throttling, or fast lanes. The gap between these positions was wide. "Both sides are still in full battle mode coming out of the FCC vote and these hearings," said Paul Gallant, a telecommunications policy analyst. "As time passes, I think both sides will see there's a

> " Why should it be the decision of Comcast or any company that the infrastructure that they happen to own in a community is good enough? Why shouldn't a community be able to say, 'We will work with another provider or work ourselves to be able to provide better infrastructure?' " [2]
>
> —Joanne Hovis, CEO of Coalition for Local Internet Choice

win-win if it's approached the right way."[3] As of October 2015, no progress had been made on the bill.

In September 2015, the Obama administration moved forward with a new broadband policy. The White House announced it wanted to upgrade the country's Internet infrastructure and promote competition among ISPs. Part of the policy endorsed the idea called "dig once," which recommends laying a single tube in the ground through which all Internet cables could pass. Then any company could add broadband cables through the same tube, opening up opportunities for new ISPs. According to the Federal Highway Administration, the concept would cut broadband installation costs by up to 90 percent.[4] The policy called for federal agencies to award grants to undertake the project.

The administration knew whatever policies Obama put into place might not last past the 2016 election if a Republican president were elected. Republican candidate Jeb Bush, for

Senator Bernie Sanders, *center*, spoke about net neutrality in early 2015 alongside Senator Al Franken, *left*, and Senator Edward Markey, *right*.

example, vowed in the Republican primary that he would dismantle net neutrality rules if he were elected president. A statement on his campaign website read, "These rules prohibit one group of companies (ISPs) from charging another group of companies (content companies) the full cost for using their services."[5] Republican candidate Marco Rubio wrote in an opinion piece that "the issue of ISPs creating different speed lanes is not the injustice that it is made out to be."[6] Democratic candidates

Hillary Clinton and Bernie Sanders were both in favor of net neutrality. Clinton wanted Internet connectivity to be treated as an infrastructure issue, and Sanders framed net neutrality as a fight against an "army of Comcast and Verizon lobbyists" who oppose rules.[7]

GLOBAL TRENDS—GAINING ACCESS

Worldwide, the trend from free and open Internet access to restricted national networks discouraged net neutrality advocates. They had hoped that as the Internet expanded to reach more isolated areas of the world, where up to 90 percent of the population was not online, net neutrality ideals would be maintained. But just gaining access in these locations is challenging.

According to *State of Connectivity: 2014*, a global report on Internet access compiled by Internet.org—an Internet connectivity company operated by Facebook—the first challenge deals with infrastructure. As in some isolated areas of developed countries,

SAUDI WOMEN ON THE INTERNET

Cultural norms in Saudi Arabia restrict women from traveling on their own and participating in male-dominated commerce. The Internet has enabled some Saudi women to start their own home-based businesses at a low startup cost. Some Saudi women operate websites for clothes, cosmetics, and food. Others have opened sites for an all-female gaming conference (GCON) and an advice and news blog for moms.

many people in undeveloped countries do not live close enough to the cables, fiber optics, and other means of providing broadband connections. The second challenge is affordability. Many people in developing countries cannot afford the cost of Internet access. The third challenge is relevance. To many people, whether in developed or undeveloped nations, the Internet is simply not relevant. They either do not know about it, cannot access Internet content in their language, or cannot read or understand the content that is there. Internet content would need to be in at least 92 languages for the Internet to be relevant to 80 percent of the world. By 2015, one of the world's most-translated websites, Wikipedia, was available in only 52 languages.[8]

BRIDGING THE ACCESS GAP

Bridging the global Internet-access gap will take a variety of solutions, some traditional and others more innovative. In developed countries, Internet access in rural areas has involved private ISPs building more cable and fiber-optic infrastructure. Some countries are building and owning their own Internet infrastructure. Others are opting for a private-public hybrid solution. In the poorest countries with the least Internet connectivity, US tech companies have introduced what they believe are unique solutions to Internet access. These solutions are not without controversy.

To reach the hundreds of millions of people without Internet access, Facebook—using its subsidiary Internet.org—has launched drones and satellites. The drones and satellites receive Internet data sent by laser beams from ground stations. Then, they send that information via laser beams to ground receivers accessible by local ISPs. Local ISPs partnering with Internet.org relay the Internet data to peoples' computers or cell phones. On July 30, 2015, Internet.org introduced its first drone, named Aquila. The aircraft—shaped like a flying wing—was solar powered and could fly for three months at a time at an altitude of 60,000 to 90,000 feet (18,000 to 27,000 m). It had the wingspan of a Boeing 737 jetliner but weighed less than 1,000 pounds (450 kg).[10] Facebook was also partnering with the French company Eutelsat to beam an Internet connection to remote parts of Africa in 2016 using Eutelsat's new AMOS-6 satellite.

In 2013, Facebook introduced Internet.org. The goal of this organization is to bring access to the Internet—using satellites, optic lasers, and even Internet-beaming drones—to the 10 percent of the world's population living in very remote areas. As of fall 2015, the company was helping 1 billion people in 19 countries in Asia, Latin America, and Africa get online.[9] Tech giant Google was also making deals in India, Africa, and other areas, offering Free Zone, which gave people up to one gigabit per month of free access to Gmail and other Google products.

Although Facebook and Google were bringing the Internet to many people for the first time, net neutrality advocates worried these giant companies were exerting too much control over what content users could access. The deals they struck with local ISPs favored Facebook and Google websites, such as Facebook news feeds, Gmail e-mail services, and Facebook and Google web searches. If a user clicked beyond these sites with their smartphones, for example, they would incur data charges. In Kenya in 2014, the top four websites were Google, Facebook, YouTube (owned by Google), and the Kenyan version of Google. Advocates also worried the huge presence of these companies kept smaller companies from entering the market, and the data Google and Facebook collected on a country's citizens might not be protected.

Net neutrality can also have a dampening effect on Internet innovation. For example, the country of Turkey offers TurkCell, a phone with talk, text, and Facebook at a price cheaper than cell phones with full Internet access. It satisfies the needs of consumers who cannot afford, or do not want, more access. But because TurkCell does not provide access to the full Internet, it would not comply with the ideals of net neutrality. It would therefore be illegal if strong net neutrality laws were put into place.

As access to the Internet grows throughout the world, the role of the Internet in everyday life will become increasingly important. So will the issue of net neutrality. Arguments continue to rage over ownership and control of the Internet.

FACEBOOK IN INDIA

To many people concerned about global Internet access, Internet.org's lofty goal of connecting "the two-thirds of the world that don't have Internet access" is a worthy one.[13] But for countries with strong support for net neutrality, such as India, it also brings up concerns of favoritism. With Internet.org, Facebook became one of only a few Internet providers in that country. Also, it partnered with only selected content providers, and net neutrality proponents feared Facebook was favoring certain websites and applications over others. Under pressure from net neutrality supporters, several Indian websites backed out of partnering with Internet.org.

As a result of that pushback from content providers and complaints from the public, Facebook decided to use a more open selection process in which any developer could "submit their site or service to us to be a part of the new Internet.org platform," said Chris Daniels, an Internet.org executive.[14] But developers would still need to adhere to some strict guidelines, which net neutrality supporters believed might limit consumers' access to content. In response to complaints, Mark Zuckerberg, CEO of Facebook, said in

internet.org

Innovation Challenge

a video post that it was "not sustainable to offer the whole Internet for free . . . but it is sustainable to build free basic services that are simpler, use less data, and work on all low-end phones."[15] The argument did not go far enough for net neutrality advocates, who became even more concerned when Facebook confirmed it would have the capability to track people who used its service.

ESSENTIAL FACTS

MAJOR EVENTS

>> The US Congress distinguished between a *telecommunications service* and an *information service* in the Telecommunications Act of 1996.

>> In 2002, the FCC ruled that cable broadband is an information service, and therefore is not subject to common-carrier regulations.

>> After evidence arose that ISPs blocked some Internet content, the FCC issued a statement listing four principles of net neutrality in 2005.

>> Comcast filed suit against the FCC in 2008, claiming the FCC does not have the right to regulate it; Comcast won the suit in 2010.

>> In February 2015, under pressure from the public, Internet content providers, and President Barack Obama, the FCC made a controversial ruling classifying all broadband ISPs as utilities subject to strict common-carrier regulations.

KEY PLAYERS

>> Law professor Tim Wu coined the term *net neutrality* in 2002.

>> FCC Commissioner Michael Powell created the four principles of the open Internet in 2004.

>> Tom Wheeler was FCC commissioner during the FCC's 2015 net neutrality ruling that categorized Internet service as a utility.

>> President Barack Obama helped sway the FCC's 2015 ruling by strongly endorsing net neutrality.

IMPACT ON SOCIETY

ISPs can limit competition and make it difficult for small web companies to find success in a number of ways. They can prevent competing ISPs from using their cables and other infrastructure; they can block or slow certain Internet traffic; and they can charge content providers an extra fee for access to Internet fast lanes. For consumers, a lack of competition among ISPs can lead to high prices and poor service. When an ISP blocks content, it can limit a consumer's complete access to information. The ISP practice of throttling—or slowing—certain content can keep consumers from getting the content they are paying for. Regulating net neutrality by classifying ISPs as utilities might result in more competition and reduce practices harmful to content providers and consumers. But regulation might also result in higher taxes for consumers, and possibly slow growth and keep ISPs from investing in infrastructure.

QUOTE

"'Net neutrality' has been built into the fabric of the Internet since its creation—but it is also a principle that we cannot take for granted."

—President Barack Obama, in a November 10, 2014, statement

GLOSSARY

ANALOG
Data expressed in a physical way, such as by the hands of a clock.

BACKBONE
A high-speed connection point between ISP servers and the infrastructure of the Internet.

BANDWIDTH
The rate at which computer data is sent from one point to another.

BROADBAND
An Internet connection operating at speeds greater than 25 Mbps.

COMMON CARRIER
A company or person who transports people or goods on regular routes at set rates.

CONSORTIUM
A group or association, usually composed of several companies.

CONTENT PROVIDER
A company that provides digital goods or services to customers on the web.

DIGITAL
Data expressed as a series of the digits 0 and 1.

INDISCRIMINATE
Random or without careful judgment.

INFRASTRUCTURE
The basic equipment and structures that are needed for a system to function properly.

MANIPULATE
To control or influence.

MONOPOLY
Exclusive control over a commodity or service.

NETWORK
A group of linked computers.

PROPONENT
A person who supports a particular theory, proposal, or policy.

SERVER
A computer that manages access to a network.

TELECOMMUNICATION
Communication over a distance, such as by telephone.

THROTTLING
Reducing power or speed.

TIER
A level or grade within a system.

ADDITIONAL RESOURCES

SELECTED BIBLIOGRAPHY

Crawford, Susan. *Captive Audience: The Telecom Industry and Monopoly Power in the New Gilded Age.* New Haven, CT: Yale UP, 2013. Print.

Lee, Timothy B. "Keeping the Internet Competitive." *National Affairs.* nationalaffairs.com, Spring 2012. Web. 11 Sept. 2015.

Wasserman, Todd. "5 Arguments Against Net Neutrality." *Mashable.* mashable.com, 16 May 2014. Web. 17 Sept. 2015.

FURTHER READINGS

Dougherty, Terri. *Freedom of Expression and the Internet.* San Diego, CA: Greenhaven, 2010. Print.

Espejo, Roman (ed.). *Should the Internet Be Free?* San Diego, CA: Greenhaven, 2010. Print.

Mooney, Carla. *How the Internet is Changing Society.* San Diego, CA: Reference Point, 2015. Print.

WEBSITES

To learn more about Essential Library of the Information Age, visit **booklinks.abdopublishing.com**. These links are routinely monitored and updated to provide the most current information available.

FOR MORE INFORMATION

For more information on this subject, contact or visit the following organizations:

Computer History Museum

1401 North Shoreline Boulevard
Mountain View, CA 94043
650-810-1010
http://www.computerhistory.org

The Computer History Museum houses the world's largest collection of computer hardware, software, and information related to the history of computing, including the history of the Internet. The museum is open to the public.

Federal Communications Commission (FCC)

445 12th Street Southwest
Washington, DC 20554
888-225-5322
https://www.fcc.gov

To tour the FCC, visitors must write a formal request letter to any FCC commissioner. Contact information can be found on the FCC website.

SOURCE NOTES

CHAPTER 1. ANYTHING BUT NEUTRAL

1. Natalie Prolman. "Something Huge Just Happened Regarding the Future of the Internet." *Global Citizen*. Global Citizen, 27 Feb. 2015. Web. 26 Jan. 2016.

2. "Last Week Tonight with John Oliver: Net Neutrality (HBO)." *YouTube*. YouTube, 1 June 2014. Web. 9 Sept. 2015.

3. Marguerite Reardon. "Net Neutrality: How We Got From There to Here." *CNET*. CNET, 24 Feb. 2015. Web. 9 Sept. 2015.

4. Elise Hu. "3.7 Million Comments Later, Here's Where Net Neutrality Stands." *NPR*. NPR, 17 Sept. 2014. Web. 10 Sept. 2015.

5. Fabienne Faur. "John Oliver, the British Comedian Spurring America to Action." *Business Insider*. Business Insider, 3 Mar. 2014. Web. 10 Sept. 2015.

6. "Last Week Tonight with John Oliver: Net Neutrality (HBO)." *YouTube*. YouTube, 1 June 2014. Web. 9 Sept. 2015.

7. Tom Risen. "The Dark Side of Net Neutrality." *US News*. US News, 1 Oct. 2014. Web. 15 Sept. 2015.

8. "Net Neutrality: President Obama's Plan for a Free and Open Internet." *White House*. White House, n.d. Web. 18 Sept. 2015.

CHAPTER 2. FROM THE EARLY INTERNET TO BROADBAND

1. Dawn C. Nunziato. *Virtual Freedom: Net Neutrality and Free Speech*. Stanford, CA: Stanford UP, 2009. Print. 120–121.

2. "History of Cable." *California Cable & Telecommunications Association*. California Cable & Telecommunications Association, 2016. Web. 26 Jan. 2016.

3. "Making the Connections." *Communications History*. FCC, 21 Nov. 2005. Web. 26 Jan. 2016.

4. Larry Downes. "After Net Neutrality Vote, an Uncertain Future for the Internet." *Washington Post*. Washington Post, 27 Feb. 2015. Web. 18 Sept. 2015.

5. "Quotes." *Techpolicy*. Techpolicy, 15 May 2014. Web. 16 Sept. 2015.

6. Dawn C. Nunziato. *Virtual Freedom: Net Neutrality and Free Speech*. Stanford, CA: Stanford UP, 2009. Print. 121.

CHAPTER 3. ISPs VERSUS THE FCC

1. Michael K. Powell. "Preserving Internet Freedom: Guiding Principles for the Industry." *FCC*. FCC, 8 Feb. 2004. Web. 18 Sept. 2015.

2. "Free Press Responds to Supreme Court Ruling in *Brand X* and *Grokster* Cases." *Free Press*. Free Press, 27 June 2005. Web. 18 Sept. 2015.

3. Peter Svensson. "Comcast Blocks Some Internet Traffic." *Washington Post*. Washington Post, 19 Oct. 2007. Web. 23 Sept. 2015.

4. "Peer-to-Peer Network." *PC Magazine*. PC Magazine, 2016. Web. 26 Jan. 2016.

5. Grant Gross. "FCC Rules Against Comcast P-to-P Throttling." *IDG News Service*. IDG News Service, 8 Jan. 2008. Web. 24 Sept. 2015.

6. Grant Gross. "Court Rules Against US FCC's Comcast Net Neutrality Decision." *PC World*. PC World, 7 Apr. 2010. Web. 26 Jan. 2016.

CHAPTER 4. THE NET NEUTRALITY PENDULUM SWINGS

1. Diane Bartz and Alina Selyukh. "Verizon, FCC Battle in Court over Net Neutrality, Site Blocking." *NBC News*. NBC News, 9 Sept. 2013. Web. 26 Jan. 2016.

2. Andrew Zajac and Todd Shields. "Verizon Wins Net Neutrality Court Ruling Against FCC." *Bloomberg*. Bloomberg, 14 Jan. 2014. Web. 21 Sept. 2015.

3. Ibid.

4. Shalani Ramachandran. "Netflix to Pay Comcast for Smoother Streaming." *Wall Street Journal*. Wall Street Journal, 23 Feb. 2014. Web. 26 Jan. 2016.

5. Jacob Kastrenakes. "FCC Scrutinizing Netflix Speed Issues on Comcast and Verizon." *Verge*. Verge, 13 June 2014. Web. 26 Jan. 2016.

6. Ibid.

7. Malarie Gokey. "FCC Net Neutrality Timeline." *Digital Trends*. Digital Trends, 12 Mar. 2015. Web. 21 Sept. 2015.

8. "Net Neutrality: President Obama's Plan for a Free and Open Internet." *White House*. White House, n.d. Web. 18 Sept. 2015.

9. "FCC Approves 'Net Neutrality' Plan to Control Internet Access." *Breitbart*. Breitbart, 26 Feb. 2015. Web. 26 Jan. 2016.

10. Rebecca Ruiz and Steve Lohr. "FCC Approves Net Neutrality Rules, Classifying Broadband Internet Service as a Utility." *New York Times*. New York Times, 26 Feb. 2015. Web. 22 Sept. 2015.

11. Ibid.

CHAPTER 5. NET NEUTRALITY SUPPORTERS

1. Max Ehrenfreund. "New Poll: Republicans and Democrats Both Overwhelmingly Support Net Neutrality." *Washington Post*. Washington Post, 12 Nov. 2014. Web. 11 Sept. 2015.

2. Allan Holmes and Chris Zubak-Skees. "US Internet Users Pay More and Have Fewer Choices than Europeans." *Center for Public Integrity*. Center for Public Integrity, 28 May 2015. Web. 14 Sept. 2015.

3. Dara Kerr. "US Download Speeds Sluggish Compared with Other Countries." *CNET*. CNET, 26 Nov. 2013. Web. 14 Sept. 2015.

4. Danielle Kehl. "New Yorkers Get Worse Internet Service than People in Bucharest." *Slate*. Slate, 21 Nov. 2014. Web. 14 Sept. 2015.

5. Allan Holmes and Chris Zubak-Skees. "US Internet Users Pay More and Have Fewer Choices than Europeans." *Center for Public Integrity*. Center for Public Integrity, 28 May 2015. Web. 14 Sept. 2015.

6. Ibid.

7. David Auerbach. "Yes, Your Internet Is Getting Slower." *Slate*. Slate, 14 May 2014. Web. 22 Sept. 2015.

8. Jon Brodkin. "Why Comcast and Other Cable ISPs Aren't Selling You Gigabit Internet." *Ars Technica*. Ars Technica, 1 Dec. 2013. Web. 22 Sept. 2015.

9. Ray Sheffer. "Which US Providers Offer the Fastest Internet Speeds?" *Yahoo Finance*. Yahoo, 3 May 2015. Web. 22 Sept. 2015.

10. Jon Brodkin. "Why Comcast and Other Cable ISPs Aren't Selling You Gigabit Internet." *Ars Technica*. Ars Technica, 1 Dec. 2013. Web. 22 Sept. 2015.

11. Cecilia Kang. "Public Interest Groups Rail Against a Comcast and NBC Merger." *Post Tech*. Washington Post, 9 Nov. 2009. Web. 26 Jan. 2016.

12. Karl Bode. "Comcast Merger Chances Stall as Regulators Realize Comcast Meddled in Hulu Management, Ignored NBC Deal Conditions." *Tech Dirt*. Tech Dirt, 22 Apr. 2015. Web. 23 Sept. 2015.

13. Andrea Caumant. "12 Trends Shaping Digital News." *FactTank*. Pew Research Center, 16 Oct. 2013. Web. 13 Sept. 2015.

14. "Last Week Tonight with John Oliver: Net Neutrality (HBO)." *YouTube*. YouTube, 1 June 2014. Web. 9 Sept. 2015.

15. Elise Hu. "3.7 Million Comments Later, Here's Where Net Neutrality Stands." *NPR*. NPR, 17 Sept. 2014. Web. 10 Sept. 2015.

16. "Artists to FCC Chairman Tom Wheeler: We've Got Your Back on Net Neutrality." *Future of Music Coalition*. Future of Music Coalition, n.d. Web. 15 Sept. 2015.

17. "Lobbyists." *Legislative Process*. US Senate, n.d. Web. 15 Sept. 2015.

CHAPTER 6. OPPOSITION TO NET NEUTRALITY

1. Larry Downes. "After Net Neutrality Vote, an Uncertain Future for the Internet." *Washington Post*. Washington Post, 27 Feb. 2015. Web. 18 Sept. 2015.

2. Thomas Mocarsky. "First Briefs Filed in Legal Challenge to FCC's Open Internet Order." *Katy on the Hill*. Katy on the Hill, 30 July 2015. Web. 26 Jan. 2016.

3. Todd Wasserman. "5 Arguments Against Net Neutrality." *Mashable*. Mashable, 16 May 2014. Web. 17 Sept. 2015.

4. Ibid.

5. Roger Yu and Mike Snider. "How Comcast, Time Warner Cable Deal Unraveled." *USA Today*. USA Today, 25 Apr. 2015. Web. 26 Jan. 2016.

6. "Press Release Telecommunications and Information 2014." *American Customer Satisfaction Index*. American Customer Satisfaction Index, 2014. Web. 14 Sept. 2015.

7. Malarie Gokey. "FCC Net Neutrality Timeline." *Digital Trends*. Digital Trends, 12 Mar. 2015. Web. 21 Sept. 2015.

8. Josh Steimle. "Am I the Only Techie Against Net Neutrality?" *Forbes*. Forbes, 14 May 2014. Web. 18 Feb. 2016.

9. "FCC Approves 'Net Neutrality' Plan to Control Internet Access." *Breitbart*. Breitbart, 26 Feb. 2015. Web. 26 Jan. 2016.

10. Mario Trujillo. "Top GOP Senator: Net Neutrality Budget Riders Unlikely." *The Hill*. The Hill, 4 Nov. 2015. Web. 26 Jan. 2016.

11. "FCC Approves 'Net Neutrality' Plan to Control Internet Access." *Breitbart*. Breitbart, 26 Feb. 2015. Web. 26 Jan. 2016.

12. Grant Gross. "Telecom Trade Group Sues FCC on Net Neutrality." *Christian Science Monitor*. Christian Science Monitor, 24 Mar. 2015. Web. 25 Sept. 2015.

CHAPTER 7. NET NEUTRALITY WORLDWIDE

1. Michael Casey. "Three-Fifths of the World Is Still without Internet." *CBS News*. CBS News, 22 Sept. 2015. Web. 28 Sept. 2015.

2. Ibid.

3. Ibid.

4. Matthew Speiser. "The 10 Countries with the World's Fastest Internet Speeds." *Business Insider*. Business Insider, 17 May 2015. Web. 14 Sept. 2015.

5. Allan Holmes and Chris Zubak-Skees. "US Internet Users Pay More and Have Fewer Choices than Europeans." *Center for Public Integrity*. Center for Public Integrity, 28 May 2015. Web. 14 Sept. 2015.

6. Danielle Kehl. "New Yorkers Get Worse Internet Service than People in Bucharest." *Slate*. Slate, 21 Nov. 2014. Web. 14 Sept. 2015.

7. Michael Casey. "Three-Fifths of the World Is Still without Internet." *CBS News*. CBS News, 22 Sept. 2015. Web. 28 Sept. 2015.

8. "About Us." *Freedom House*. Freedom House, n.d. Web. 1 Oct. 2015.

9. "Global Threats to Net Neutrality." *New York Times*. New York Times, 10 Apr. 2015. Web. 15 Sept. 2015.

10. "Freedom on the Net 2014." *Freedom House*. Freedom House, n.d. Web. 1 Oct. 2015.

CHAPTER 8. THE FUTURE OF NET NEUTRALITY

1. Susan Crawford. *Captive Audience: The Telecom Industry and Monopoly Power in the New Gilded Age*. New Haven, CT: Yale UP, 2013. Print. 254–255.

2. Vauhini Vara. "Why the FCC's Municipal-Broadband Ruling Matters, Too." *New Yorker*. New Yorker, 28 Feb. 2015. Web. 8 Oct. 2015.

3. Jim Puzzanghera. "Potential for a Bipartisan Bill on Net Neutrality Emerges in Congress." *Los Angeles Times*. Los Angeles Times, 25 Mar. 2015. Web. 26 Jan. 2016.

4. Brian Fung. "Dig Once: The No-Brainer Internet Policy the White House Just Endorsed." *Washington Post*. Washington Post, 22 Sept. 2015. Web. 12 Oct. 2015.

5. Chris Welch. "Jeb Bush Would Wipe Out the FCC's Net Neutrality Rules if Elected President." *Verge*. Verge, 22 Sept. 2015. Web. 12 Oct. 2015.

6. Caroline Craig. "Where the Candidates Stand on Net Neutrality." *InfoWorld*. InfoWorld, 25 Sept. 2015. Web. 26 Jan. 2016.

7. Caroline Craig. "Where the Candidates Stand on Net Neutrality." *InfoWorld*. InfoWorld, 25 Sept. 2015. Web. 26 Jan. 2016.

8. "State of Connectivity: 2014." *Internet.org*. Internet.org, n.d. Web. 7 Oct. 2015.

9. Lonnie Shekhtman. "Facebook's Quest for Universal Internet Access: Next Stop, Sub-Saharan Africa." *Christian Science Monitor*. Christian Science Monitor, 5 Oct. 2015. Web. 26 Jan. 2016.

10. Zach Miners. "Meet Aquila, Facebook's Unmanned Internet Drone." *PC World*. PC World, 30 July 2015. Web. 26 Jan. 2016.

11. "The State of Broadband 2015." *Broadband Commission*. Broadband Commission. Sept. 2015. Web. 7 Oct. 2015.

12. Ruth Alexander. *BBC News*. BBC News, 29 Mar. 2012. Web. 9 Feb. 2016.

13. Tess Danielson. "Facebook Opens Up Internet.org Amid India's Battle for Net Neutrality." *Christian Science Monitor*. Christian Science Monitor, 5 May 2015. Web. 28 Sept. 2015.

14. Ibid.

15. Ibid.

INDEX

ABOUT THE AUTHORS

Melissa Higgins writes fiction and nonfiction for children and young adults. Two of her novels for struggling readers, *Bi-Normal* and *I'm Just Me,* are silver-medal winners in the Independent Publisher (IPPY) Book Awards. Higgins' nearly 40 nonfiction titles range from character development and psychology to history and biographies. When not writing, Higgins enjoys hiking and taking photographs around her home in the Arizona desert.

Michael Regan, MEd, worked for 30 years as a middle-school and college counselor and advisor before turning his attention to research and writing. He is especially interested in topics related to technology and current events. He lives in the southwest.